D1561731

	DATE DUE		

LOOKING INTO THE PAST:
PEOPLE, PLACES, AND CUSTOMS

Scottish Clans and Tartans

by

Dwayne E. Pickels

Chelsea House Publishers

CHELSEA HOUSE PUBLISHERS

Editor-in-Chief Stephen Reginald
Managing Editor James D. Gallagher
Production Manager Pamela Loos
Art Director Sara Davis
Picture Editor Judy Hasday
Senior Production Editor Lisa Chippendale
Designer Takeshi Takahashi

First Printing

1 3 5 7 9 8 6 4 2

Library of Congress Cataloging-in-Publication Data

Pickels, Dwayne E.
Scottish clans and tartans / by Dwayne E. Pickels.

p. cm. — (Looking into the past)
Includes bibliographical references and index.
Summary: Examines the history of Scotland's clans by estab-
lishing their origins, probing the highpoints of their heyday,
considering alignments among them, and identifying their
mottoes.

ISBN 0-7910-4676-1

1. Clans—Scotland—Highlands—Juvenile literature. 2. Tartans—Scotland—Highlands—Juvenile literature. 3. Highlands (Scotland)—Civilization—Juvenile literature.
[1. Clans. 2. Tartans. 3. Scotland.] I. Title. II. Series.
DA880.H76P53 1997
941.1'5—dc21   97-23451
                                                    CIP
                                                    AC

CONTENTS

CULTURE, CUSTOMS, AND RITUALS

The important moments of our lives—from birth through puberty, aging, and death—are made more meaningful by culture, customs, and rituals. But what is culture? The word *culture,* broadly defined, includes the way of life of an entire society. This encompasses customs, rituals, codes of manners, dress, languages, norms of behavior, and systems of beliefs. Individuals are both acted on by and react to a culture—and so generate new cultural forms and customs.

What is custom? Custom refers to accepted social practices that separate one cultural group from another. Every culture contains basic customs, often known as rites of transition or passage. These rites, or ceremonies, occur at different stages of life, from birth to death, and are sometimes religious in nature. In all cultures of the world today, a new baby is greeted and welcomed into its family through ceremony. Some ceremonies, such as the bar mitzvah, a religious initiation for teenage Jewish boys, mark the transition from childhood to adulthood. Marriage also is usually celebrated by a ritual of some sort. Death is another rite of transition. All known cultures contain beliefs about life after death, and all observe funeral rites and mourning customs.

What is a ritual? What is a rite? These terms are used interchangeably to describe a ceremony associated with a custom. The English ritual of shaking hands in greeting, for example, has become part of that culture. The washing of one's hands could be considered a ritual which helps a person achieve an accepted level of cleanliness—a requirement of the cultural beliefs that person holds.

The books in this series, *Looking into the Past: People,*

Places, and Customs, explore many of the most interesting rituals of different cultures through time. For example, did you know that in the year A.D. 1075 William the Conqueror ordered that a "Couvre feu" bell be rung at sunset in each town and city of England, as a signal to put out all fires? Because homes were made of wood and had thatched roofs, the bell served as a precaution against house fires. Today, this custom is no longer observed as it was 900 years ago, but the modern word *curfew* derives from its practice.

Another ritual that dates from centuries long past is the Japanese Samurai Festival. This colorful celebration commemorates the feats of the ancient samurai warriors who ruled the country hundreds of years ago. Japanese citizens dress in costumes, and direct descendants of warriors wear samurai swords during the festival. The making of these swords actually is a separate religious rite in itself.

Different cultures develop different customs. For example, people of different nations have developed various interesting ways to greet each other. In China 100 years ago, the ordinary salutation was a ceremonious, but not deep, bow, with the greeting "Kin t'ien ni hao ma?" (Are you well today?). During the same era, citizens of the Indian Ocean island nation Ceylon (now called Sri Lanka) greeted each other by placing their palms together with the fingers extended. When greeting a person of higher social rank, the hands were held in front of the forehead and the head was inclined.

Some symbols and rituals rooted in ancient beliefs are common to several cultures. For example, in China, Japan, and many of the countries of the East, a tortoise is a symbol of protection from black magic, while fish have represented fertility, new life, and prosperity since the beginnings of human civilization. Other ancient fertility symbols have been incorporated into religions we still practice today, and so these ancient beliefs remain a part of our civilization. A more recent belief, the legend of Santa Claus, is the story of a kind benefactor who brings gifts to the good children of the world. This story appears in the lore of nearly every nation. Each country developed its own variation on the legend and each celebrates Santa's arrival in a different way.

New rituals are being created all the time. On April 21, 1997, for example, the cremated remains of 24 people were launched into orbit around Earth on a Pegasus rocket. Included among the group whose ashes now head toward their "final frontier" are Gene Roddenberry, creator of the television series *Star Trek,* and Timothy Leary, a countercultural icon of the 1960s. Each person's remains were placed in a separate aluminum capsule engraved with the person's name and a commemorative phrase. The remains will orbit the Earth every 90 minutes for two to ten years. When the rocket does re-enter Earth's atmosphere, it will burn up with a great burst of light. This first-time ritual could become an accepted rite of passage, a custom in our culture that would supplant the current ceremonies marking the transition between life and death.

Curiosity about different customs, rites, and rituals dates back to the mercantile Greeks of classical times. Herodotus (484–425 B.C.), known as the "Father of History," described Egyptian culture. The Roman historian Tacitus (A.D. 55–117) similarly wrote a lengthy account about the customs of the "modern" European barbarians. From the Greeks to Marco Polo, from Columbus to the Pacific voyages of Captain James Cook, cultural differences have fascinated the literate world. The books in the *Looking into the Past* series collect the most interesting customs from many cultures of the past and explain their origins, meanings, and relationship to the present day.

In the future, space travel may very well provide the impetus for new cultures, customs, and rituals, which will in turn enthrall and interest the peoples of future millennia.

Fred L. Israel
The City College of the City University of New York

CONTRIBUTORS

Senior Consulting Editor FRED L. ISRAEL is an award-winning historian. He received the Scribe's Award from the American Bar Association for his work on the Chelsea House series *The Justices of the United States Supreme Court*. A specialist in early American history, he was general editor for Chelsea's *1897 Sears Roebuck Catalog*. Dr. Israel has also worked in association with Dr. Arthur M. Schlesinger, jr. on many projects, including *The History of U.S. Presidential Elections* and *The History of U.S. Political Parties*. They are currently working together on the Chelsea House series *The World 100 Years Ago*, which looks at the traditions, customs, and cultures of many nations at the turn of the century.

DWAYNE E. PICKELS is an award-winning reporter with the *Greensburg (Pa.) Tribune-Review*. A Magna Cum Laude graduate of the University of Pittsburgh, where he cofounded the literary magazine *Pendulum*, Dwayne won a Pennsylvania Newspaper Publishers' Association (PNPA) Keystone Press Award in 1992. He currently resides in Scottdale, Pa., with his wife, Mary, and their daughter, Kaidia Leigh. In his free time, he is currently immersed in a number of literary pursuits—which include a novel based on Celtic myth and legend. In addition to writing, Dwayne enjoys outdoor excursions, including bird watching, hiking, photography, and target shooting…along with typically futile attempts at fishing.

Overview
Scottish Clans and Tartans

For what basically amounts to half an island in the northern reaches of the Atlantic Ocean, the lush and lively history of Scotland may well rival that of almost any nation in its cultural diversity and splendor. Packed with brave heroes and legendary figures, the story of the proud Scots and their struggles has captured the fascination of many throughout the centuries.

But perhaps no singular aspect of Scottish history has earned so celebrated an image as that of its unique and colorful clan system. Wielding two-handed Claymores and ornate basket-hilted swords, these fierce and clever Highland clans often proved as formidable a foe to each other as to any invading force. It is likely this was one reason the tartan system was developed—the ability to distinguish a fellow clansmen from a foe with a glance at a kilt serves to some advantage on the field of battle. In more modern times, the highly individualized colors and weave patterns that served to identify one clan from another play more ceremonial and sentimental roles, and they are sometimes extremely far-reaching sources of ancestral pride (Neil Armstrong took a piece of his family's tartan with him on his historic first walk on the moon).

However, while these specialized garments may prove sufficient fodder for a complete and exhaustive work in itself, the story of the people who once donned them is perhaps of greater importance. After all, clothes don't really make the person...do they? And so it is with such motivation that we briefly examine the colorful history of Scotland's clans by probing several major highpoints of their heyday in history. First, we will attempt to establish origins, and finally, identify the illustrious mottos associated with each clan. In between, we'll take a look at the alignments of each during several of Scotland's major efforts to attain independence from England—conflicts that elevated the clans to prominence and, ultimately, delivered their demise as a social system.

STEWART,
PRINCE CHARLES EDWARD

STEWART

The Stewart (or later, Stuart) dynasty of Scottish Kings hails from a Norman line that came to England with William the Conqueror. Walter Fladd, who arrived in Scotland with King David I in the early 1100s, was named its "Steward" and given estates in Renfrewshire and East Lothian.

In the late 13th century, a descendant, James, the fifth High Steward, swore allegiance to King Edward I of England but later joined William Wallace in the fight for Scotland's independence. At Wallace's death, the Stewart clan sided with Robert the Bruce, who had taken up that cause. Walter, the High Steward, later married the Bruce's daughter, Marjorie, securing a kingship for his son after the heirless death of the Bruce's only son, David II. Sir Walter's son, the Bruce's grandson, Robert Stewart, ruled as Robert II. His son, John, is said to have taken the name Robert III because John was the name of an English king and also of a Scottish claimant to the throne. But for the rule of Mary Queen of Scots in the 1500s, the family's male line held the throne until the ascension of Queen Anne in 1714. Born in 1720, Prince Charles Edward Louis Philip Casimir Stewart—also known as "Bonnie Prince Charlie," "the Young Pretender" or "the Young Chevalier"—attempted to regain his family's throne, which led to the downfall of many Highland clans, and, some say, to the clan system itself.

In addition to the royal line, there were also three other main branches of Stewarts during the 14th and 15th centuries: the Appin, Atholland, and Balquhidder branches. Several mottos are attributed to the Stewarts, including *nobilis est ira leonis,* meaning, "noble is the wrath of a lion," and *virescit vulnere virtus,* which means, "courage gains strength from a wound."

SCOTT.

SCOTT

Two principal houses of the Clan Scott—the Scotts of Balweary (Fife) and the Scotts of Buccleuch (Selkirk)—are said to have descended from two sons of an Uchtred, known as "son of the Scot," who witnessed charters in the early 12th century.

In a roundabout way, a member of the clan played a unique role in the country's history. It seems that after the death of King Alexander III in 1286, it was a Michael Scott of Balweary who was dispatched to Norway in 1290 to escort the king's granddaughter, Margaret, "the Maid of Norway," back to Scotland. However, when the child heir to the Scottish crown died en route, succession to the crown was laid open to more than a dozen claimants, and King Edward I of England was invited to arbitrate a successor. Ruthlessly using the situation to its fullest advantage, Edward went on to assume control of Scotland, plunging the clans into the Wars for Independence in 1296.

Another source cites a Sir Michael Scott, the second Laird of Buccleuch, as being a staunch supporter of Robert the Bruce, who subsequently assumed Scotland's crown. By the end of the 15th century, the Scotts had become one of the most powerful of the feuding Border clans.

One of the clan's most famous sons was Sir Walter Scott (1771-1832). But it was less for his title as the first Laird of Abbotsford than for his role as a prolific poet, novelist, historian and folklorist. Sir Walter Scott is responsible for a great deal of the Highland clan and tartan images that permeate modern literature. He is perhaps best known for his 1818 work that immortalized the legendary escapades of Rob Roy MacGregor.

The Scott clan motto is *Amo*, which is Latin for, "I love."

MACGREGOR.

MACGREGOR

Clan MacGregor is probably the most well known of the Highland clans due to the legendary Rob Roy MacGregor, immortalized in novel by Sir Walter Scott. However, despite Rob Roy's heroic status—and a motto, *S rioghal mo dhream*, which means, "royal is my race"—the sons of Scotland have historically been less than abiding to this heralded clan.

King Robert the Bruce plunged the MacGregor clan into a tumultuous conflict when he gave the barony of Loch Awe (which included much of the MacGregor land) to the Campbells for helping him to the throne in the 14th century. This forced the clan deeper into its territories, restricting them to the region of Glenstrae. It also led to at least 10 years of warfare in the 1500s that reduced the clan's members to outlaw status.

In 1603—after a Royal forester was killed in retaliation for hanging a band of MacGregors caught poaching—King James IV ordered the clan to be abolished, which meant members were forced to renounce their name or die. A MacGregor chief and nearly a dozen of his chieftains were then hung in Edinburgh, leaving the rest of the clan to scatter and assume other Highland names to conceal their lineage and avoid being hunted down like animals.

The MacGregors became known as "children of the mist." Even Rob Roy, born in 1671, had to assume his mother's name (Campbell) in order to survive and become a thorn in the government's side until his death in 1734. The edict abolishing the MacGregor clan was repealed by King Charles II out of gratitude to MacGregor clansmen who fought against Cromwell, but it was later reimposed when William of Orange took the throne and was not repealed permanently until 1774.

MACNEILL.

MacNeill

Clan MacNeill claims lineage from one Niall—
a descendant of Aodh O'Neil, who was said to
have ruled in northern Ireland during the
early 11th century. Aodh was a descendant of
a fifth century pagan who founded the mighty U'Neill
dynasty and came to the island of Barra in the Outer
Hebrides around 1049.

Neil MacNeill, fifth Laird of Barra, was a prince of the
Council of the Isles in 1252 and was chief when Haakon
IV's army was defeated at Largs in 1263, ending Norse rule
of the Hebrides. His son, Neil Og MacNeill, is believed to
have fought with Robert the Bruce at Bannockburn in 1314
during the War for Independence against King Edward I
("Longshanks") of England, and he was subsequently
rewarded with more lands in northern Kintyre.

Another branch of MacNeills was established on the
island of Gigha under Torquil MacNeill in 1427 and
opposed the Barra MacNeills during a feud between the
MacDonalds of Isaly and MacLeans of Duart.

The MacNeills were said to have been steadfast Jacobites. After fighting for James VII at Killiecrankie in 1689,
the clan remained loyal to the Stewart cause, rallying to the
"Young Pretender" in the uprising of 1715. It was also sym-
pathetic to the Jacobites' cause in 1745. However, unlike
many of its fellow clans, MacNeill managed to keep its
estates in that struggle's aftermath.

Also said to be famous for its maritime prowess and for
lawlessness on the high seas, the MacNeill clan's motto,
Buaidh no bas, means "to conquer or die." An old Highland
saying claims the Biblical Noah is not found among Mac-
Neill lineage because "MacNeill had a boat of his own."

FERGUSSON.

FERGUSSON

The origin of the name Fergusson (*MacFhear-guis* in Gaelic, meaning, "son of Fergus") has been said to trace to the founder of one of Scotland's early monarchies—Fergus, who lived in Ireland around 300 B.C. Research done around the 13th century by medieval historians confirms that a group of people, led by a descendent, the Irish King Fergus Mor mac Erc, left Northern Ireland and settled in Dalriada around A.D. 500. The region later became known as Argyllshire.

Later, the clan reportedly dispersed from Argyll and spread into other regions of the country. Prior to the 18th century, at least five groups of Fergussons possessed lands in Argyll, Perthshire, Aberdeenshire, Dumfriesshire, and Aryshire, where they lived as separate clans. Present day Fergussons still own extensive lands in Ayreshire and Balquhidder.

There were said to have been "Sons of Fergus" allied with Robert the Bruce during the Wars for Independence—including a John, son of Fergus, who witnessed a charter between the Bruce and King Edward II of England signed at Turnberry following the battle at Bannockburn in 1314. Some Perthshire Fergussons are also said to have stood with James Graham, the fifth Earl of Montrose in 1644, and Fergussons are noted as ardent supporters of the Jacobite causes in 1715 and 1745. Numerous political, religious, and cultural achievements are also attributed to the clan's members. The literary work of a Robert Fergusson, who died in 1774, is said to have been greatly revered by Scotland's premier poet, Robert Burns.

The Fergusson motto, *Dulcius ex asperis,* means: "Sweeter after difficulties."

CAMPBELL
OF BREADALBANE.

CAMPBELL OF BREADALBANE

Breadalbane is one of three major houses under the surname Campbell, which most likely derived from the Gaelic *cam-beul,* meaning "twisted mouth." The Campbell clan is said to be one of the oldest in the Highlands. Some sources cite the first Campbell in written record as a Gillespie in 1263. However, others credit a 1386 crown charter with acknowledging Duncan MacDuihbne as founder of the Campbells, who were established as the Lords of Loch Awe. Most authorities tend to agree it is from this line that Breadalbane Campbells are descended, particularly from a Colin Campbell, son of Sir Duncan Campbell of Loch Awe.

In 1432, Colin obtained the lands of Glenorchy, after which the family quickly prospered. In 1445, Sir Duncan Campbell of Loch Awe was named Lord Campbell, and his grandson and heir, also named Colin, later became the first Earl of Argyll. Argyll's uncle, yet another Colin, founded a line that rivaled Loch Awe in splendor—the Earls of Breadalbane. Other factions became the Earls of Cawdor and Loudoun.

Though the Campbells are regarded as steadfast supporters of the Crown throughout the 15th century, an internal rivalry for chieftanship among the various houses is said to have led to a feud that nearly split the clan in the century that followed. In the 1700s, Campbells are listed as supporters of English government, fighting against the Jacobites in the uprisings of 1715 and 1745.

Mottos attributed to the clan are: (Argyll) *Ne obliviscaris,* Latin for "Forget not"; (Breadalbane) "Follow me"; (Cawdor) "Be mindful"; and (Loudoun) "I bide my time."

GRANT.

GRANT

Some sources claim the Clan Grant was a principal branch of the great Clan Alpin—the Highland clan whose chiefs are said to have descended from King Alpin, father of Kenneth MacAlpin, the first king of the Scots. However, others report the name can be traced to a Norman lineage, deriving the name from the Norman French *le grand,* meaning "great" or "large." Grants are also said to be of the same stock as the Clan Gregor.

The clan first appears on record in the mid–13th century, when it acquired lands in Stratherrick through marriage. Its support of Robert the Bruce during the Wars for Independence against England in the late 13th and early 14th centuries confirmed its holdings in Strathspey. So, despite any apparent conflict over its origin, the Clan Grant was well established as influential in northeast Scotland, along with other clans of Anglo-Norman descent, such as the Camerons and the Frasers.

Like the latter, the Clan Grant sided with the House of Hanover (King George I and II of England) in the civil wars (Jacobite uprisings) of 1715 and 1745, although some of its individual members are said to have remained loyal to the movement to shed England's control and return the Scottish throne to the Stewart Kings.

In Gaelic, the name for Grant is *Grandd.* One Grant motto (and war cry) is listed as "stand fast," while another is given as *Craig Elachie,* meaning, "the rock of alarm."

MACPHERSON.

MACPHERSON

eaning "son of the parson," the origin of this clan's name may sound generic enough. However, the traditional history and genealogy of Clan MacPherson apparently traces to one specific Celtic clergyman—a Gilliecatton Mor. It is said that from this grandson of Muireach (or Murdoch) Cattenach, who became the Parson of Kingussie in Badenoch, followed the family name of Mac-a-Phersain ("the son of the parson"), which later developed into MacPherson. It's also commonly held that the clan was one of the earliest, if not most ancient, families of fabled Clan Chattan, a conglomeration of clans dating to the 15th century.

The clan's principal family was the MacPhersons of Cluny. As was the case with many clans, the MacPhersons' territory of Upper Speyside was granted to the family in the early 1300s in return for service to Robert the Bruce (for whom they later fought at Bannockburn). The MacPhersons helped to drive the Bruce's enemies, the Comyns, from Badenoch. Thus the "Sons of the Parson" became neighbors to the MacKintoshes of Moy. A subsequent marriage between the two clans is said to have been the basis for a dispute over chieftainship of the Clan Chattan confederation.

Cited as keen Jacobites, the MacPhersons, like many Highland clans loyal to the House of Stewart, suffered for that allegiance and lost many of their former estates—most of which, however, were subsequently restored in 1784.

The MacPhersons are sometimes called the Clan of the Three Brothers, after the three sons of Ewan Ban MacMhuirich: Kenneth of Cluny, Iain of Pitmain and Gillies of Invereshire.

"Touch not the cat but a glove" is the MacPherson motto.

MATHESON.

MATHESON

ne of the most powerful families in northern Scotland, the Clan Matheson claims descent from the Celtic Earls of Ross, who granted it lands in the Lochalsh, Lochcarron, and Kintail regions. Another principal family of Mathesons hailed from Shiness in Sutherland.

MacMathans, as they were originally known, were settled in Lochalsh in Wester Ross from an early period. Kenneth MacMathan, constable of Eilean Donan, is recorded in the Norse account of the expedition of King Haakon IV against Scotland in 1263. Despite the subsequent victory over Haakon at Largs, it is also commonly assumed there was some intermingling of Norse blood within the clan.

Mathesons fought for Donald of the Isles at Harlaw in 1411, and they were later caught in the midst of a bitter feud between the MacDonalds and the MacKenzies. In 1427, a Chief Alastair Matheson was arrested at Inverness and was later beheaded at the order of James I in Edinburgh. Alastair had two sons—John, who spawned the Mathesons of Lochalsh, and Donald Bain, from whom came the Sutherland Mathesons. A Donald Matheson of Shiness fought against the Jacobites in the uprising of 1715.

The name Matheson is attributed to one of two possible Gaelic translations, *Mic Mhathghamhuin'*, meaning, "son of the bear," and *MacMhathain,* meaning, "son of the heroes." There are also Lowland and English (Mathison) derivations of the name that translate simply as, "son of Matthew."

The motto of the Mathesons of Lochalsh is *Fac et spera,* which means, "Do and hope."

MACRAE.

MacRae

settling in the Kintail region of Wester Ross during the 14th century, Clan MacRae is said by some historians to have previously originated from the lands of Clunes near Beauly during the 12th and 13th centuries.

Some 400 years later, during the 16th century, the MacRaes earned the label of "the MacKenzies' shirt of mail" for their staunch support of the MacKenzies of Kintail. It was also around that time, in 1539, that a constable of Eilean Donan Castle named Duncan is credited with ending a siege by the MacDonald clan on the MacKenzie stronghold by slaying the opposing host's chieftain with an arrow. For this, he received title to the lands of Inverinate, and the clan later obtained the title "Earl of Seaforth" as well as the hereditary constableship of Eilean Donan Castle.

Alongside their MacKenzie brethren, the MacRaes were said to have distinguished themselves with bravery and military prowess during first of the Jacobite uprisings of the early 18th century, primarily during their fight for the Stewart cause at Sheriffmuir. And though they did not take part as a clan in the second uprising in 1745, many individual MacRaes are said to have been among those who supported Prince Charles Edward Stewart's effort to return Scotland to his family's rule.

With a Celtic name that stems from a Gaelic phrase meaning, "son of grace," the motto of the MacRaes of Inverinate is *Fortitudine,* which means, "with fortitude."

MACDUFF.

MacDuff

The Cross of MacDuff stands in the northeast region of Fife, near Newburgh. According to ancient tradition, any kinsman of the MacDuffs wanted for a crime could claim sanctuary at the cross—though some say such claim is only intended for cases of unintentional homicide. Nonetheless, it may go a long way toward explaining the MacDuff motto: *Dues juvat* ("God assists").

The Clan Duff, as MacDuff originates, is said to claim its descent from the royal Scoto-Pictish line through Queen Gruoch, the wife of MacBeth. Tradition has it that a Mac-Duff clansman who opposed MacBeth and aided Malcolm III in seizing the throne of Scotland in the second half of the 11th century was in turn made the first Earl of Fife. From that time, members of Clan MacDuff have enjoyed the privilege of crowning Scotland's kings and leading the nation's army, thus the popular phrase, "Lead on, MacDuff."

Though the MacDuff Earls of Fife long played a prominent role in many early Scottish historical affairs, the family is not as prominent in more recent periods of Scotland's history. Some sources indicate the old earldom of Fife ended in 1353 with the death of the 12th Earl, Duncan. Others say it was forfeited for treason in 1336 and was passed to Robert Stewart, who subsequently became Duke of Albany and Regent of Scotland.

In the centuries that followed, though, a number of separate families of Duffs and MacDuffs resurfaced and claimed lineage from the earlier clan. In the early 1900s, the dukedom of Fife passed to the chiefs of the Carnegies through marriage.

DUNCAN.

DUNCAN

The history of Clan Donnachaidh is more well known as the Clan Robertson. To dispel confusion, it must be explained that the clan takes its name from an early chieftain named Duncan, who was the fifth in descent of Conan of Glenerochie, a younger son of Henry, Earl of Atholl. Also known as "Fat Duncan," this chieftain led the clan at Bannockburn in 1314, in support of Robert the Bruce. The clan continued to be known as Duncan until around 1450, when it adopted the name Robert, after a king who captured two of King James I's assassins.

In addition to the clan's claim of descent from the ancient Earls of Atholl, several other accounts of the Duncan (Robertson) origin are given from an obscure early history. One is that it descended from the MacDonald clan; another is that they belonged to the line of Columba, and thus were of early Irish (Fergus) nobility.

In the 1600s, the Robertsons supported Charles I, following Montrose in all of his campaigns. The clan later showed Jacobite loyalty in 1715 (joining the Earl of Mar), and again in 1745, under "Bonnie Prince Charlie." Nonetheless, the Robertsons are said to be one of the few Jacobite clans who could claim the good fortune of going relatively unpunished in the aftermath, despite such continued service to the House of Stewart.

The clan's principal land holdings were on Loch Tay and Loch Rannoch, though branches of the clan reached further north into Inverness-shire.

The motto *virutis gloria merces,* which means, "glory is the reward of valor," is attributed to the Robertson Clan.

MACLEOD.

MacLeod

Clan MacLeod hails from the islands of Lewis and Skye, as well as several areas of the mainland of northwest Scotland. The originator of this clan is cited as Leod—whose father, Olaf the Black, was one of the last Norse kings of the Northern Isles. Leod inherited Lewis and parts of Skye upon his sire's death in 1237. Through marriage, the clan later acquired Dunvegan Castle in northern Skye, which remains the family's seat in the modern day.

Two principal branches of this clan descended from two of Leod's sons, Siol Tormod (the MacLeods of Harris and Skye) and Siol Torquil (the MacLeods of Lewis).

The MacLeods followed the MacDonald Lord of the Isles in the 15th century—though they managed to escape the wrath of King James IV during his attempt to break the MacDonalds' stronghold. Later, the direct line of the Lewis branch ended and its estates were passed to the MacKenzies and Mathesons. However, occupying MacKenzie chiefs continued to call their seat "Castle Leod."

Though they are listed as supporters of the Stewarts, some sources claim the Clan MacLeod was forced to "sit out," so to speak, during the first Jacobite uprising in 1715, after losing more than 500 clansmen to Lord Protector Oliver Cromwell's forces in the late 1600s. The MacLeods later viewed Bonnie Prince Charlie's plan to retrieve the crown in 1745 as ill-conceived and thus declined to participate in the battle at Culloden during that conflict.

The mottos of the Clan MacLeod were "Hold Fast" (Harris), and "I shine, not burn" (Lewis).

OGILVIE.

OGILVIE

ccording to some sources, the name of this clan is derived from the Gaelic *Mac Ghille Bhuidhe,* while others report it comes from the Old English word, *Ocel-fa,* which means "high plain."

Nonetheless, the Clan Ogilvie is said to hail from the lands of Ogilvie in Forfarshire, which was once a Pictish kingdom. Its chiefs are believed to have descended from Gillebride, one of the ancient Celtic nobles of Scotland who became the first earls. Gillebride, the second son of Ghillechriost, Earl of Angus, bestowed the lands of Ogilvie and Easter Powrie on his younger son, Gilbert, around 1177, after he was granted a barony by William the Lion in 1163.

Ogilvies were the hereditary sheriffs of Angus in the 14th and 15th centuries. A Sir Patrick Ogilvie commanded the Scottish forces with Joan of Arc against the English. Sir Walter Ogilvie, son of Ogilvie at Wester Powrie, was appointed Lord High Treasurer of Scotland in 1425. Five years later, he served as ambassador to England. A long line of Ogilvie descendants experienced similar prosperity and high status until around 1639.

From that time on—until some level of restoration was enacted in the late 18th century—the Ogilvies suffered numerous losses and hardships for its allegiance to the Stewarts' cause, as was the fate of many of the Jacobite Highland clans who remained loyal to the Stewart Kings in the earlier half of the 1700s.

Such loyalty lends credence to the motto attributed to the Ogilvie Clan: *A Fin,* which means, "To the End."

MACKENZIE.

MacKenzie

Clan MacKenzie is said to be descended from Gillean of the Aird, a 12th-century ancestor of the Earls of Ross. By the early 1200s, the clan had settled at Eilean Donan castle. Built on a rocky island at the mouth of Loch Duich, the mighty stronghold faces the island of Skye to the west.

Among that settlement was a Kenneth, who is also credited as the source of the modern translation of MacKenzie, "son of Kenneth." MacKenzies are of Celtic stock, unlike some of the neighboring clans of Norman ancestry. Although subordinate to the MacDonalds throughout their early history, the MacKenzies later rose to become one of the most powerful clans in the north.

The Kintail (which is Gaelic for "head of the sea") region they originally inhabited in Ross-shire includes virtually all the types of terrain that can be found in Scotland. The clan later expanded its domain, eventually reaching the east coast and finding fertile fields and meadows along the way.

By the early 17th century, their territory stretched from the Black Isles to the Outer Hebrides. However, because of MacKenzie's support of the House of Stewart, that changed in the early 1700s, when the clan lost its lands and titles in the aftermaths of the Jacobite uprisings.

Two mottos attributed to this clan are: *Luceo non uro,* which means "I shine, not burn" (also the motto of the Lewis branch of the MacLeods), and, more appropriately in light of its Stewart loyalties, *Cuidich'n righ,* which translates as "Help the King."

MACIVOR.

MacIvor

The name for this clan is said to have been derived from the Gaelic *Maciomhar,* meaning, "son of Ivar," which sources indicate is a Norse name.

Nonetheless, as we have seen with the Duncan and Robertson clans, Clan MacIvor (also MacIver) is closely— and often indiscriminately—associated with the Campbell clan, and both were intertwined with the great house of Argyll throughout much of the 17th and 18th centuries.

Going back further in time, it is said that one Iver Crom possessed lands in Argyllshire and conquered the lands of Cowal for King Alexander II in the 13th century. MacIvers also held estates at Asknish, with deeds binding them to use the name, though they remained closely allied with the Campbells.

During the Jacobite civil wars of the early 1700s, Campbells were among those who supported the central governments of Kings George I and II of England, whose thrones Argyll helped to retain against rising Jacobite forces. This support helped amass the clan's power and fortune in the aftermath of the decisive battle at Culloden in 1745, which sounded the death knell to clanship as a working social system.

In more modern times, the compound name MacIver-Campbell was used among the clan's principal houses. An active society that was established at Strathendry Castle in Fife presently strives to promote awareness of the distinct character of the family name, lending credence to the MacIvor Clan motto: *Nunquam obliviscar,* which means, "I will never forget."

SINCLAIR.

SINCLAIR

t. Clair in Pont d'Eveque in Normandy is credited as the birthplace of this clan, though the territorial home of Clan Sinclair was said to have been Caithness. In Argyllshire, and elsewhere in the west of Scotland, a branch of this clan was known by the Gaelic designation *Clann-na-Cearda,* which means "children of the craft." The term is said to have been coined for the clan's principal occupation of metal-working. In other parts of Scotland, the name takes the form of St. Clair.

One of the earliest records of the name in Scotland is found in 1162, when Henry de St. Clair received a charter to lands of Herdmanston near Haddington. The St. Clairs of Herdmanston were created peers with the title Lord Sinclair in 1449, and the line flourishes to the present day.

Chiefs in other lines of the clan descended from Sir William Sinclair, a sheriff of Edinburgh, who was granted the barony of Roslin in 1280. William's grandson, Henry, became Earl of Orkney through his mother, Isabel. Henry was credited with conquering the Faroe Islands in 1391 and also with the discovery of Greenland. More recently, historians have come to believe that he may have voyaged as far as the Americas, possibly landing in both Nova Scotia and Massachusetts.

Family debt resulted in mortgaging the Sinclair family estates to the Campbells in the late 17th century. And though they were later retaken by force, a great number of Sinclairs were slain. The Sinclair earldom was later reinstated by an order of Parliament in 1681.

The Clan Sinclair motto is: "Commit thy work to God."

FARQUHARSON.

FARQUHARSON

Throughout its colorful history, Clan Farquharson has lived up to its motto—"By Fidelity and Fortitude," as translated from the Latin, *fide et fortitudine*—standing among the most faithful and loyal to the House of Stewart.

In earlier times, outnumbered by some of its more predatory Aberdeenshire neighbors, the Farquharsons became part of the fabled confederation of clans known as Chattan.

Bearing a fierce reputation that left them known as "the fighting Farquharsons," they fought under Montrose in 1644 and formed part of the Scottish army under Charles II at Worcester in 1651. In 1689, they joined forces under the Viscount of Dundee for James VII, led by a John Farquharson of Inverey, who was known as "the Black Colonel." At the outbreak of rebellion against the Treaty of Union, they are said to have been the first of the Jacobites to muster at the summons of the Earl of Mar in the cause of 1715. At the subsequent battle of Sheriffmuir, when the Scottish army was defeated at Preston, John Farquharson of Invercauld, a colonel in Clan Chattan, was taken prisoner and held in London for some 10 months. However, this did not dismay the Farquharsons, who once again supported "Bonnie Prince Charlie," occupying the battleline's center with other Clan Chattan members at the Battle of Culloden in 1746.

The clan's name is of Celtic origin. Currently, the Farquharson estate covers some 200,000 acres of wooded moor in the Grampian region of Aberdeenshire.

BUCHANAN.

BUCHANAN

uth chanain is the Gaelic phrase that means, "house of the cannon." Some sources cite the earliest family of this name as hailing from the shores of Loch Lamond, a territory granted by the Earls of Lennox to a man named Absalon around 1225. Other sources indicate this ancient clan takes its name from the lands of Buchanan in Stirlingshire, and it is said they held extensive possessions in the Loch Lamond district for centuries.

Nonetheless, Absalon is said to have possibly been a clergyman, or at least to have been from a family dedicated to service of the ancient Celtic Church.

In 1282, a Morris of Buchanan received a charter confirming his lands with baronial rights. He also held the small island of Clarinch—the name of which later became a battle cry for his clan. The Buchanans supported the cause of Robert the Bruce in the Wars for Independence, and, as with many other highland clans, subsequent victory in that effort helped to secure the family's fortunes. However, at the death of a chief in 1682, the ancient Buchanan lands were supposed to have passed to Buchanan of Arnprior, but instead were sold to meet heavy debts. There has not been a recognized chief for this clan since the late 17th century. Of note, however, is that James Buchanan was the 15th president of the United States.

Mottos listed for the Clan Buchanan are: *Audaces juvo,* which is Latin for, "I help the brave," and *clarior hinc honos,* which is Latin for, "brighter the honor hence."

MACFIE.

MACFIE

here are evidently numerous theories surrounding the origin of the Clan Macfie. In modern Gaelic form, the name is *Maca'phi.* Celtic legend claims it is descended from a seal-woman who was prevented from returning to the sea. However, other sources cite the name as derived from *MacDhuibhshith,* which means "son of the dark faery." In Galloway, the name reportedly took the form of Macguffie, and Machaffie. On the tiny island of Iona, there is said to be a tombstone in honor of Malcolm MacDuffie, who married the sister of one of the most powerful 15th-century chieftains of the clan Donald. Nonetheless, the Clan MacFie—also known as Macphee, Macafie, or Macduffie—is said to be a branch of the Clan Alpin, which settled on Colonsay.

Located off western Argyllshire, the island is held as the clan's original home and is said to have remained in its possession until some time in the 17th century, when it passed to the MacDonalds, and later, to the MacNeills. While remnants of the clan later spread to Lochaber and other districts, the Macphees of Colonsay are credited as the hereditary keepers of the records of the Lords of the Isles.

While the motto of the Clan Macfie is *Pro rege,* which means, "for the king," sources say the clan became splintered and dispossessed. Some members were said to have followed the MacDonalds of Islay; others settled in Cameron lands, under Lochiel, following the Stewart (Jacobite) cause to the ill-fated battle of Culloden in 1746.

In the mid-19th century, one Evan Macphee became known as "the last Scottish outlaw"—living with his rebellious band and family on an island in Loch Quoich and recognizing no law.

CAMERON
OF LOCHIEL.

CAMERON OF LOCHIEL

amerons were one of the last to don kilts bearing their clan's colors in battle—during World War II. Among a number of theories behind the origin of the Cameron name, one has the clan claiming descent from a son of Camchron, a king in Denmark. Another, more accepted, hypothesis is that an early chief of the clan, Donald Dubh, came from the medieval family of Cameron of Ballegarno of Fife. It is said that Donald Dubh married an heiress of the MacMartins of Letterfinlay and later united the confederation of tribes that became known as the Clan Cameron in the 1400s. Their lands at Lochiel were united by charter as a barony in the 16th century, around the time of a Cameron chief known as Ewan MacAllan.

One source credits a descendant of Ewan, known as "Gentle Lochiel," with facilitating the 1745 Jacobite uprising by allowing the natural charm of Prince Charles Edward Stewart to win his (and the clan's) allegiance. It is said that if Lochiel had not come out in support of Bonnie Prince Charlie, that second bloody rebellion might never have occurred. However, the Camerons, which had previously outlasted the onslaught of Cromwell's forces, had already long been strong supporters of the Stewarts—as one of the mottos attributed to the clan alludes: *Mo righ's mo dhuchaich,* Gaelic meaning "for king and country." And though the clan's role in the uprising of 1745 resulted in the forfeiture of estates (as was the fate of a number of loyal Jacobites), they were subsequently restored.

Another motto ascribed to the clan is *Aonaibh ri cheile,* which is Gaelic for, "Unite."

GORDON.

GORDON

Said to have wielded such enormous power during the 16th and 17th centuries that their chief was often referred to as the Cock of the North, Clan Gordon emerged from the Lowlands in the 14th century and went on to become one of the most powerful clans in northeast Scotland.

While most sources agree the clan was originally of Anglo-Norman descent, the name Gordon is said to have been derived from the parish of Gordon in Berwickshire and one Sir Adam de Gordon, who was granted Strathbogie after the Aberdeenshire territory was confiscated from the Earl of Atholl. This was no doubt a reward for staunch support of Robert the Bruce's cause—which included being one of several ambassadors sent to Rome in the 14th century to petition the Pope to remove an excommunication that had been placed upon the Bruce. The king had earned the penalty by slaying a rival inside a church.

In the 15th century, the Gordon clan became embroiled in a struggle between the crown and the Douglasses. The Gordons allied with the royals, and in retaliation an ally of the Douglasses devastated the clan's lands and burned its castle at Huntley after Gordon's soldiers ventured south to aid the king. However, when the Douglasses were defeated, Castle Huntley was rebuilt from the rubble of the old one, and the new castle was the equal of any of the great halls of the realm.

Two mottos attributed to the Clan Gordon are *Bydand,* which means, "Abiding" or "Remaining," and *Animo non atitia,* which translates, "By courage, not cunning."

ROSS.

ROSS

Clan Ross hails from the district of the same name, which is located in the northwestern region of Scotland's mainland, east of the island of Skye. The Rosses occupied the peninsula between the Cromarty and Dornoch firths, a district that was more agricultural than pastoral and said to have been quite fertile. While the clan claims descent from the ancient Celtic Earls of Ross, they are also known in the Highlands as *Clann Gillie Aindrais,* "the children of Andrew."

For his distinguished service in crushing a rebellion in Moray in the early 1200s, it is held that Sir Farquhar Mac an t-Sagairt (son of the priest), the hereditary Abbot of Applecross, was named the first Earl of Ross by Alexander II.

William, the third Earl, led the clan at Bannockburn under Robert the Bruce during the War for Independence in 1314 and signed the Declaration of Arbroath in 1320, marking Scotland's fleeting freedom from England. Later in the 1300s, two primary branches of the Ross clan are said to have emerged: the Rosses of Balnagowan and the Rosses of Rariches.

Nearly 1,000 Ross clansmen are reported to have been among the royalists who stood against Cromwell at the battle of Worcester in 1651. However, the clan as a whole is regarded as having avoided participation in the Jacobite uprisings of 1715 and 1745, although at least one individual clan leader is said to have joined Price Charles Edward in the latter conflict.

The motto attributed to the Clan Ross is *spem successus alit,* which translates "success nourishes hope."

MACMILLAN.

MACMILLAN

esearch reveals two prevalent theories as to the Clan MacMillan's origin, which may well both be correct. The earlier of the two lists the clan as descended from one of the ancient tribes of northern Picts. While they claimed Moray as the district of their origin, they apparently also were a nomadic lot. The other theory associates MacMillans with the Celtic Church in the early 12th century—and more particularly, to a peculiar hairstyle.

Corman, a Celtic priest appointed by Alexander I as bishop of Dunkeld, had numerous sons. One, Gillie Chriosd, is said to have been the progenitor of the MacMillans. As a Celtic priest, the bishop's son would have had a distinctive "tonsure," which meant his hair was shaved from the front of his head, rather than the Roman method of shaving a ring around the crown. The Celtic tonsure was described as that of St. John, which is translated in Gaelic as *Mhaoil-Iain.* From this comes MacMillan, or "one who bore the tonsure of St. John." An alternate form is *MacGhillemhaoil,* or "son of the tonsured servant," as favored by the Lochaber branch of the clan.

A MacMillan chief, Maolmuire, is said to have sheltered Robert the Bruce when he was forced into hiding in the Highlands. The clan also fought alongside the Bruce at Bannockburn in 1314.

Two of the most enduring MacMillan memorials include a round tower near Castle Sween, which is known as MacMillan's Tower, and a Celtic cross in the churchyard at Kilmory.

The motto attributed to the Clan MacMillan is *Miseris succurrere disco* ("I learn to succor the distressed").

KENNEDY.

KENNEDY

Some sources attribute the name of Clan Kennedy to the less-than-flattering old Irish word *cinneidigh,* which translates literally as "ugly headed." However, under other Gaelic interpretations, such as *Ceannaideach,* the clan's origin seems to be northern Ireland, from where the founders of this clan sailed to settle in the ancient region of Dalriada, which later became known as Strathclyde. There, they were said to have been led by one Gilbert, whose son, Duncan, became the first Earl of Carrick in Ayrshire in the 12th century.

The Kennedy clan supported the Bruce in a conflict with the Comyns in the late 1200s, as well as during the Wars of Independence in the early 1300s, and were thus rewarded. Around 1360, a John Kennedy became the owner of lands at Cassillis, and in 1457, his descendant, another Gilbert, was made Lord Kennedy. His younger brother James was the Bishop of St. Andrew's and later founded Scotland's first university, which bears the same name. In 1509, the third Lord Kennedy became the first Earl of Cassillis.

In the 15th century, an Ulric Kennedy is said to have fled Ayrshire for Lochaber to evade prosecution under the law. There, he initiated the Clan Ulric, from which came the Kennedys of Skye—families that later became a sect of Clan Cameron.

Hugh Kennedy of Ardstinchar, one of many Scots who fought for the French through the Auld Alliance, was a commander under Joan of Arc against the English at the siege of Orleans.

The motto attributed to the Clan Kennedy is *Avise la fin,* which means "consider the end."

IMPORTANT DATES IN THE HISTORY OF SCOTLAND AND ITS CLANS

81 A.D. – The first written record of Scotland is created by the Roman historian Tacitus.

121 A.D. – Roman Emperor Hadrian orders the construction of a defensive wall stretching from Solway Firth to Tyne to keep the raiding northern tribes out of the Roman province of Britain.

4th century – Rome abandons outposts in Scotland and Britain. Celtic Scots from northern Ireland have already begun colonizing regions of Argyll, Kintyre and other parts of the Kingdom of Dalriada in the west. Picts have settled in the northern regions of "Alba" (the old name of Scotland). In the east and south, territories are held by Celtic Britons and Teutonic Anglo-Saxon tribes.

6th century – Irish missionary-statesman St. Columba establishes a monastery at Iona in 563, marking the birthplace of the Celtic Christian Church in Scotland and the subsequent end of paganism. By the seventh century, all four kingdoms of Alba are converted to Christianity.

8th–9th centuries – Norsemen begin to invade Scotland, conquering Ornkey, Shetland and the Western Isles. Faced with a common foe, the kingdoms achieve some measure of unity. In 843, Kenneth MacAlpin becomes the first monarch to rule Scotland, crowned King of the Scots of Dalriada.

13th–14th centuries – Following several hundred years of struggles between the emerging clans, along with external strife and negotiations with Norway and Britain, King Edward I ("Longshanks") of England lays claim to Scotland with occupying forces. In 1297, a commoner, William Wallace, initiates and leads a resistance force that draws warriors from all parts of Scotland, winning a decisive battle at Stirling that same year. A year later, though, in 1298, Wallace's forces are soundly defeated at Falkirk by English troops led by Longshanks himself. In 1305, he is captured by Edward's troops and executed in London, but the Wars for Independence continue under the leadership of Robert the Bruce, who crowns himself King of Scots in March 1306. Edward's death in 1307 proves a turning point; his weak successor, Edward II, later abandons most efforts to keep Scotland after a bitter defeat at Bannockburn in 1314, though conflicts simmer for nearly two more decades. Robert the Bruce dies of leprosy at the age of 53 in 1329. Later, Scottish rule is assumed by Robert Stewart (the Bruce's grandson) upon the death of the Bruce's only son, David. Though the Stewarts hold the throne for many generations, Scotland again falls to English rule through invasion, treacherous political maneuvering, and weakening of the clans through continued warfare.

17th-18th centuries - After the Dutch usurper William of Orange is proclaimed King of England, Ireland, and Scotland in 1689, a group of Highlanders known as Jacobites rise in opposition to a foreign despot. Though their rebellion is quelled before the end of the 1700s, the Jacobites arise again following an unpopular Treaty of Union signed with England. In 1715, after George I of Hanover is named king in Edinburgh, some 12,000 armed Jacobite clansmen are raised in an unsuccessful attempt to restore Scottish rule to Prince James Edward Stewart. When the revolt fails, Stewart flees to France and the clans that supported him lose their titles and estates. In 1745, Prince Charles Edward Louis Philip Casimir Stewart ("Bonnie Prince Charlie") attempts to regain the throne; however, the failed effort, culminating in the Battle of Culloden in 1746, again leads to the downfall of many Highland clans.

19th-20th centuries - As the dawn of industrialization, trade, and technology results in an eventual general apathy toward violent separation from the Union, Scotland later goes on to achieve some level of administrative independence through political means.

INDEX ⊞